Contents

A sky full of stars

Wild and Free

Once I was young

Dreams Dark Dance

Healing Me

Brown Eyes

Drunk

Seascape

Connections

Messy Minds

Autumn Leaves

Growing up

Paradise

Poetic Tapestry

Hopeful Dreams Unite

Whispers of time

In the tapestry of time, a thread so fleet,
Swiftly woven through moments, ever discreet.
Like shadows chasing the setting sun's glow,
The years rush by like a river in constant flow.
Oh, how swiftly the sands of time slip away.

Like autumn leaves dancing in a gusty ballet.
Weaving through the seasons, they silently pass.
Leaving behind memories, a fleeting contrast
Once tender sprouts, now towering trees,
The years have flown by on whispers and pleas.
Each dawn is a reminder of moments we've lost.
Yet filled with the hope of what lies beyond the frost.

From the innocence of youth to wisdom's embrace,
Time paints our lives with its swift, artful pace.
Like sparrows taking flight, forever on the wing,
Years blend into one another like a seamless string.
The cradle of spring gives way to summer's heat.
Then autumn's hues, a masterpiece so sweet
And in winter's frost, we find solace and peace.
As the years weave their tale, yearning for release.
Oh, how the years blur and blend into one!

Tears Beauty

In the realm of emotions, where tears reside,
There lies a truth that cannot be denied.
For within the depths of sorrow's embrace,
Crying emerges with its own grace.

Let not the world proclaim it as weak,
For in vulnerability, strength does peak.
Each tear that falls, a story it tells,
Of resilience, healing, and where pain dwells.

When storms of life unleash their might,
And burdens weigh heavy, clouding our sight,
The act of weeping becomes a sacred art,
A release of emotions, a mending of heart.

Through shimmering droplets, emotions flow,
Cleansing the soul, like rivers that bestow,
A catharsis profound, a gentle relief,
As tears carry solace, beyond belief.

In sorrow's tapestry, tears weave a thread,
Stitching together the words left unsaid.
They speak of love lost and dreams unmet,
Of triumphs and failures we can't forget.

For tears are but whispers of the soul,
Expressing the depths that words can't control.
They soften the edges of anguish and strife,
Allowing the spirit to find its own life.

So let the tears fall, like rain from the skies,
For within each teardrop, beauty lies.
In vulnerability's embrace, we find our worth,
And discover the strength to heal the earth.

Embrace the tears, let them shimmer and glow,
For crying is okay, and beautiful, you know.
In every drop shed, a story takes flight,
Bathed in the moon's glow, as stars ignite.

So weep if you must, let your tears dance free,
For crying is a testament to humanity.
In the ebb and flow of emotions we find,
That tears, like life's symphony, intertwine.

Thoughts

In the silence of contemplation's embrace,
Thoughts bloom like flowers with delicate grace.
They wander through realms of imagination's delight,
Shaping narratives, painting colors bright.

From the depths of thought, knowledge is born,
A tapestry of ideas, intricately woven and worn.
They shape the course of our lives, you see,

Molding our reality, defining our destiny.
Yet thoughts can also be tempests, fierce and wild,
Storms of doubt and fear that leave us beguiled.
But even amidst chaos, there is wisdom to glean,

For thoughts hold the power to heal and redeem.
So cherish the magic that thoughts bestow,
Let them guide you, like a compass, wherever you go.
For within their realm, possibilities unfold,
And the wonders of the mind's landscape behold.

Loving Me

I paint my flaws with shades of grace,
Embracing scars as part of my embrace,
For perfection's mirage, a fleeting illusion,
True beauty lies in self-acceptance's fusion.

With every breath, I inhale self-worth,
Exhaling judgments, unleashing rebirth,
For in this vessel, this vessel called "me,"
Resides the power to set my spirit free.

I dance to the rhythm of self-compassion,
Unfolding petals of love in every fashion,
Each day, a new verse in this symphony,
Celebrating the essence that makes me me.

Oh, how sweet it is to love oneself,
To cherish the soul, treasure one's wealth,
For in this love, a boundless energy thrives,
Igniting the fire that forever strives.
So I shall love myself, fiercely and true,
Embracing the light that in me imbues,
In this dance of self-love, I find my way,
Unveiling the majesty of each passing day.

Sun, Sand, Sea's Burning

Beneath the summer sun's fervent gaze,
I dance upon the sands ablaze.
Bronze-kissed skin, the fiery art,
The sun's embrace, igniting my heart.

Sea whispers secrets as waves crash near,
A symphony of bliss, both far and clear.
Salt-kissed breeze, a gentle song,
Serenading souls where dreams belong.

With every ray, a tale unfolds,
A love affair, untamed and bold.
The sun's caress, a burning desire,
Ignites my spirit, sets my soul on fire.

In this realm where summer reigns,
I find solace, as my spirit gains.
Beneath the sun, the sand, the sea,
I'm bound to freedom, wild and free.

Shadows in the twilight

In the twilight's embrace, where shadows reside,
A melancholic tapestry, life's bitter stride.
Amidst the symphony of laughter and strife,
We tread upon this stage, the theater of life.

We dance on fragile strings, our hearts intertwined,
Yet sorrow's sweet melody remains unconfined.
For life, dear friend, is a wistful lament,
A journey of shadows, where joys may be spent.

We search for solace in fleeting moments of bliss,
Yet find ourselves trapped in a world of abyss.
The seasons change, as do the tides of our souls,
And melancholy echoes through the stories life unfolds.

Oh, how we yearn for the warmth of the sun,
But find comfort in the darkness when all is done.
For it is in our sorrow that we truly feel alive,
In the bittersweet melodies that help us survive.

Sunset Chase

Across horizons vast, my heart takes flight,
With nimble steps, I embrace the fading light,
In pursuit of colors that paint the sky,
I chase the sunsets, as they bid goodbye.

Through meadows ablaze with amber fire,
I chase the sunsets, my sole desire,
Each stride adorned with hope's tender grace,
To capture the essence of heaven's embrace.

With every stride, a symphony awakes,
Celestial notes, each melody partakes,
Whispering secrets in the zephyr's sigh,
As I chase the sunsets, beneath the sky.

In hues of coral, and shades of crimson fire,
The sun dips low, a celestial choir,
A tapestry woven with ethereal thread,
As I chase the sunsets, where dreams are bred.

Oh, the secrets the sunsets seem to hold,
As if eternity's story they unfold,
Each stroke of color, a chapter untold,
In this grand tapestry of life we behold.

With outstretched arms, I reach for the sublime,
Casting away the constraints of space and time,
The fading sun kisses the edge of the earth,
As I chase the sunsets, my heart rebirthed.

Though they may elude my ardent quest,
Like fleeting moments, they put me to the test,
I'll never cease pursuing their elusive grace,
Chasing sunsets, in this enchanted chase.

For in the pursuit, I find solace and peace,
A gentle release, my weary soul finds ease,
In the symphony of colors, my spirit flies,
Chasing sunsets, under heaven's watchful eyes.

So I'll follow their trail, wherever it may lead,
Across oceans vast, or atop mountains freed,
For in the chase, I discover my own worth,
Chasing sunsets, upon this blessed Earth.

A nighttime spell

In the heart of night's enchanting domain,
Lies Light City, where dreams and radiance reign.
Neon hues paint a tapestry of delight,
As stars and moon cast their shimmering light.

Skyscrapers soar, touching the midnight sky,
Their glass facades reflecting secrets held high.
Bridges span rivers, their arches aglow,
Guiding wanderers in the city's nocturnal flow.

Silhouettes dance amidst the soft moonbeams,
Whispering secrets in a realm of dreams.
Laughter echoes, filling the city's embrace,
Creating an ambiance impossible to erase.

Light City, a haven where reality transcends,
A symphony of luminescence that never ends.
In this realm, shadows come alive,
A celestial canvas where dreams thrive.

Womanhood

In the realm where strength and grace converge,
Where femininity blooms with a gentle surge,
A tapestry of wonders, a soul's vibrant hue,
I celebrate the essence of being a woman true.

Embrace, dear sister, your divine birthright,
For you are a beacon, a radiant light,
Through trials and triumphs, you have grown,
A masterpiece of resilience, beautifully sown.

In the depths of your spirit, a symphony resides,
A melody of courage, where self-love abides,
Unveil the layers, shed doubt and fear,
Embrace your reflection with love sincere.

For you are the embodiment of fierce might,
A force of nature, a celestial flight,
Your curves and contours, each line and scar,
Tell tales of wisdom, stories that spar.

In loving yourself, you blossom like a flower,
A testament to strength, in every waking hour,
Your soul dances freely, unshackled and unbound,
A testament to the power that is profound.

Embrace the softness, the whispers in your veins,
Celebrate your passions, embrace your pains,
For in every moment, you're a masterpiece divine,
A tapestry of beauty, adorned in love's design.

So let the world witness your radiant soul,
As you navigate the tides, both gentle and bold,
Unapologetically, you stand, in your truth and grace,
A woman fierce and loving, shining in every space.

So, my dear sister, hear this truth I proclaim,
You are worthy, deserving of love's sweet acclaim,
Embrace the woman within, in all her splendid glory,
And watch her flourish, the heroine of her story.

Boyfriends Laundry

His scent, oh, his scent, like a whispered desire,
It sets my soul ablaze, igniting a fire.
It weaves through the air with an alluring grace,
A symphony of notes, creating a magical chase.

At first, it's a whisper of crisp morning dew,
Fresh and invigorating, like skies azure blue.
Hints of citrus linger, a burst of sunshine bright,
Awakening senses with each breath, like a flight.

In his smell, I find whispers of forgotten dreams,
Unspoken words, and love's gentle streams.
It's a language unspoken, a secret connection,
A fragrant symphony of profound affection.

So I breathe him in, his scent like a spell,
Lost in the magic that only he can compel.
For his smell is a melody, a symphony divine,
A love song in whispers, forever entwined.

Raindrops

Raindrops dance upon my windowpane,
Tiny messengers from the silver-gray sky.
Each one carries a tale of its journey,
Whispering secrets as it passes by.

With gentle taps, they create their own song,
A symphony of nature's sweetest refrain.
Their rhythm lulls me into a tranquil state,
As I listen to their melodic domain.

I watch them race, chasing one another,
Leaving trails of liquid pearls in their wake.
They unite and separate with graceful ease,
Creating patterns I can't help but partake.

Each raindrop a prism, reflecting the light,
A kaleidoscope of colors, pure and bright.
They paint a picture on my glass canvas,
A masterpiece that's ever-changing in sight.

Sometimes they trickle, a soft serenade,
Other times they cascade, a fierce ballet.
Yet in their dance, they bring a certain calm,
An invitation to dream and simply sway.

They blur the world beyond, like a gentle haze,
As if to shield me from life's transient strife.
And in their presence, I find solace,
In the gentle rhythm of this transient life.

So let the raindrops tap upon my window,
Their symphony of nature's sweet embrace.
For in their dance, I find a moment's respite,
A tranquil haven in this hectic space.

Raindrops on my window, delicate and free,
You bring comfort and peace, a soothing decree.
As I sit and marvel at your whispered tales,
I'm reminded of the beauty in life's details.

Real is rare

In a world of masks and hidden faces,
Where authenticity is lost in empty spaces,
I stand amidst a crowd, yet I feel alone,
Yearning for truth, a place to call my own.

In a realm where facades are carefully crafted,
I choose to be genuine, untamed and unshafted,
My heart beats fiercely with raw honesty,
A beacon of truth in this sea of fallacy.

While others chase hollow accolades and fame,
I find solace in being true, staking no claim,
I'd rather be an island in a sea of deceit,
Than lose my essence, surrender, and retreat.

I seek connections that run deep and true,
Eyes that reflect souls, genuine and blue,
For amidst the fakery, I yearn for kinship,
A tribe of kindred spirits, a real friendship.

Globetrotter's Journey

In distant lands where dreams unfurl,
I wandered 'neath a boundless sky,
With heart alight, and spirit free,
Embarking on a journey to see.

Through winding paths and unknown shores,
I sailed across the ocean's roar,
With every wave that kissed the prow,
A new horizon seemed to grow.

In ancient cities steeped in tales,
I walked the streets where history prevails,
Each cobblestone a whisper old,
Stories of triumph and tales untold.

The scent of spices filled the air,
As bazaars beckoned with treasures rare,
Colors vibrant, a tapestry grand,
In markets bustling, hand in hand.

I climbed the mountains, kissed by snow,
To gaze upon the valleys below,
Nature's majesty, awe-inspiring,
A world of wonders, never tiring.

I stood in awe of ancient ruins,
Witnessing empires once so grand,
Their remnants whispering secrets old,
Of triumphs, defeats, and tales untold.

Through rolling meadows, flowers dance,
As gentle breezes sing and prance,
Embracing lands of untamed grace,
Nature's canvas, a masterpiece.

I mingled with souls from distant lands,
United by a traveler's bands,
Shared laughter, stories, and a smile,
For in our hearts, the world compiled.

With every step, my perspective grew,
The world's vast tapestry in view,
And as I wandered, unconfined,
I found myself, with newfound mind.

For in these travels far and wide,
I found my place, my joy, my stride,
A world of wonders, waiting there,
For those who seek, who dare to care.

Parisian Serenade

In Paris, where love's whispers fill the air,
Romance dances upon cobblestone streets.
The city of dreams, a tapestry rare,
Where hearts entwine in passion's sweet retreats.

Beneath the moonlit glow of Eiffel's might,
Lovers stroll along the Seine's gentle flow.
Their laughter and kisses, a symphony bright,
As Parisian nights embrace love's afterglow.

In quaint cafes, where fragrant lattes brew,
Couples linger, lost in each other's gaze.
Their hands entwined, a bond forever true,
They share secrets whispered in love's haze.

Oh, Paris! The city of amour's delight,
Where dreams are born and destinies entwine.
Romance ignites in every flickering light,
As love's flame burns, a passion so divine.

Life's Best Treasures

Gaze upon the morning sun, as it paints the sky,
A golden brushstroke of warmth, bidding darkness goodbye.
The gentle touch of a loved one, a tender embrace,
An unspoken language of love, filling every space.

In laughter's sweet symphony, hearts find their release,
Unleashing joy's melody, bringing souls at peace.
The vibrant hues of nature, a canvas divine,
Where blooms dance in harmony, an ode to life's design.

A stranger's act of kindness, a beacon of light,
Restoring faith in humanity, dispelling the night.
The embrace of friendship, steadfast and true,
A shelter in life's storm, when skies turn dark blue.

The whispers of wisdom, carried on gentle breeze,
Guiding us through the labyrinth, with grace and ease.
The taste of simple pleasures, on our lips they reside,
A sip of coffee's warmth, a moment we can't hide.

The exhilaration of discovery, as knowledge unfurls,
Unveiling secrets of the universe, in endless swirls.
The pursuit of dreams, with unwavering might,
Igniting hope within, a beacon in the night.

And in the quiet solitude, when day turns to rest,
Reflection takes its hold, offering solace and zest.
For in these cherished moments, we find our truest selves,
Where life's essence whispers, revealing hidden wells.

So cherish these treasures, the best things we hold dear,
For they are the essence of life, to keep forever near.
In the tapestry of existence, they paint a masterpiece,
The best things in life, woven with love, and never cease.

A sky full of stars

Amongst the twinkling chorus, there's a star,
A radiant emblem from afar.
It whispers of courage, of unwavering belief,
A gentle reminder of life's sweet relief.

With every shimmering star that graces the sky,
A reminder that hope shall never die.
Through life's trials and shadows we tread,
Stars of resilience illuminate the thread.

They teach us to embrace the darkest hour,
For hope's eternal light has boundless power.
In the night's embrace, we find solace and grace,
A tapestry of stars, hope's eternal embrace.

So let the night unfold its stellar tale,
And let our hearts, like shooting stars, prevail.
For within each luminary gleam that gleams,
Hope awakens, transcending our wildest dreams.

Wild and Free

In a realm where boundaries dissolve,
I wander as a creature untamed,
Where the winds whisper secrets old,
And the universe calls my name.

I run with the rivers, swift and clear,
Their currents carry my unbounded soul,
In their depths, my inhibitions disappear,
As I embrace nature's sacred role.

In the wilderness, my heart takes flight,
In harmony with creatures of the wild,
With fiery eyes, I chase the moon's light,
Unleashing the untamed, fierce and wild.

So let the winds carry my untamed song,
Across mountains and oceans vast,
In this vast universe, I truly belong,
As a wild and free spirit, forever to last.

Once I was young

Once I was young, a tender soul,
With dreams untamed, my heart aglow.
In innocence, I danced and played,
A world of wonder, where time delayed.

The sun would rise in golden hues,
Birds would sing, spreading joyful cues.
I chased the breeze, with laughter's glee,
Imagination set my spirit free.

The meadows beckoned, with blossoms rare,
Colors vibrant, perfumed the air.
I'd weave my dreams among the flowers,
Lost in moments, cherished for hours.

Oh, how the world was full of grace,
Every day, a new adventure to embrace.
I'd climb the trees, touch the sky,
Believing dreams would never die.

But seasons change, as time goes by,
Youth's sweet innocence begins to fly.
The shadows lengthen, doubts creep in,
And life's complexities, they do begin.

Once I was young, with stars in my eyes,
Believing in love, beneath moonlit skies.
But hearts can break, and dreams can fade,
Leaving scars upon the paths we've made.

Yet within me, a flicker remains,
A spark of hope that forever sustains.
Though innocence lost, and trials endured,
I find solace in memories treasured.

For once I was young, and now I am wise,
With lessons learned from life's demise.
Through joy and sorrow, I've come to know,
Strength arises, even as shadows grow.

So let the years advance with pace,
I'll embrace each line upon my face.
Once I was young, and now I am strong,
Ready to face whatever may come along.

Dreams Dark Dance

Within this ethereal theater of the night,
Visions emerge, casting a chilling, eerie light,
They dance in whispers, conjuring fears untold,
Unleashing torrents of dread, relentless and bold.

Oh, bad dreams, how you weave your wicked tales,
In the recesses of minds, like haunting trails,
You manifest as demons with fiery eyes,
And nightmares that torment beneath moonlit skies.

From the depths of darkness, you rise, unbidden,
A symphony of anguish, where hope is hidden,
In twisted landscapes, surreal and surreal,
Where fears take form and wounds refuse to heal.

So, bad dreams, I'll confront your spectral might,
With courage and resolve, I'll seek the light,
For in the realm of dreams, where nightmares roam,
I'll find solace, and turn a house into a home.
And when the morning sun, in golden rays, does gleam,
I'll rise from slumber's depths, escaping your bad dream.

Healing me

In the depths of sorrow's darkest night,
Where anguish lingers, consuming light,
There lies a path, both gentle and wise,
To mend your heart, to heal its cries.

Like fragile petals, tender and weak,
Your wounded heart seeks solace, it seeks
A balm to soothe the ache, to make it whole,
To nurture seeds of hope within your soul.

Embrace the silence, let it gently sway,
For in its arms, tranquility holds sway.
In whispers soft, your heart shall find release,
As healing melodies sing sweetly, bringing peace.

Let nature's canvas be your sanctuary,
Where vibrant colors paint a tapestry
Of beauty, reminding you of life's embrace,
Renewing faith, revealing endless grace.

Seek solace in the touch of gentle hands,
Hands that hold you, understand your demands.
Let their warmth seep through every crack,
Binding wounds, bridging the love you lack.

Release the burdens that weigh upon your chest,
The memories that haunt, refusing to rest.
In forgiveness, find liberation's sweet release,
And watch your heart blossom, finding inner peace.

Time, the gentle healer, softly mends,
Stitching the fragments as patience extends.
Embrace its rhythm, let it guide your way,
For with each passing day, healing finds its stay.

And when the scars have faded, leaving traces,
A testament to strength, and life's graces,
Your heart shall emerge, resilient and whole,
A beacon of light, a testament to your soul.

So let the tears flow, cleansing the pain,
As healing waters wash away the strain.
For in surrender, you shall find rebirth,
And witness the miracle of your heart's worth.

Heal, dear heart, with courage as your guide,
Embrace the journey, let love reside.
In every mended piece, a story shall be told,
Of how you conquered darkness, and your spirit bold.

Brown Eyes

In those depths of mystery, his eyes reside,
A gateway to a realm where secrets hide.
Like celestial orbs, they shimmer and gleam,
Enchanting all who dare to meet their beam.

Within those irises, a tale unfolds,
Whispering stories of wonders untold.
A palette of hues, a symphony of light,
They dance and dazzle, a captivating sight.

His eyes, like windows to a soul unseen,
Reflect the joys and sorrows life has been.
With every glance, emotions intertwine,
Revealing the depths of a love divine.

Those eyes, like beacons, guide me through the night,
Igniting hope, dispelling any fright.
They hold the power to heal and to mend,
A gentle touch, a message they send.

Drunk

The amber liquid swirls in my glass,
Whispering secrets of a love that won't pass.
Intoxicated, my heart starts to sway,
In a dance of emotions, I cannot betray.

His laughter echoes in the chambers of my mind,
A symphony of joy, so rare to find.
His eyes, like stars, once bright and true,
Now lost in shadows, my heart breaks in two.

With each sip, I'm pulled into a trance,
A wistful longing, a bittersweet chance.
The drunken haze blurs reality's line,
And I'm lost in the depths of love's red wine.

In this inebriated state, I reminisce,
About stolen moments, an intoxicating kiss.
The touch of his hand, like a burning flame,
Ignites a desire I cannot tame.

But the alcohol-induced reverie soon fades,
Reality crashes in like ocean waves.
I'm left with the ache of a love that's gone,
Drunk and alone, in the early dawn.

Yet, in the depths of the whiskey's embrace,
I find solace, a fleeting sense of grace.
For in drunken stupor, I can pretend,
That he still lingers, my heart's true friend.

So I raise my glass, a toast to the past,
To love's elixir, fading too fast.
In the haze of a drunken night's whim,
I'll always think of him, my thoughts not dim.

Seascape

Born from winds that roam the sea,
They rise and fall in perfect spree,
Their mighty crests, they reach so high,
Caressing heavens with a lullaby.

A ballet of foam upon the shore,
As waves in harmony gently roar,
Their restless spirits never cease,
Embracing secrets, finding peace.

With graceful curves, they ebb and flow,
Like liquid poetry in a mystical show,
They whisper stories from distant lands,
Carving tales in soft, shifting sands.

They carry dreams from distant shores,
Unfolding mysteries, unlocking doors,
Their timeless rhythm, a sacred song,
Guiding souls where they belong.

Connections

In the labyrinth of human connections, we tread,
Where emotions entwine, intricate and widespread,
A tapestry of complexities, woven with care,
Let me paint a verse, the tale we often share.

Two souls dance upon a stage of intrigue,
A delicate balance, love's eternal league,
They intertwine like vines, entangled and vast,
Bound by desires that forever will last.

Their hearts, once entwined in harmonious song,
Now sing a tune that feels undeniably wrong,
In the depths of their bond, shadows arise,
A symphony of contradictions, love's disguised.

Passion turns to anger, words cut like blades,
Misunderstandings weave darkened cascades,
A tango of emotions, where laughter meets tears,
Their path, once clear, now cloaked in fears.

They drift in an ocean of uncertainties and doubts,
Lost in a maze of silence, love's whispers turned shouts,
Yet amidst the chaos, a spark remains,
A glimmer of hope, refusing to wane.

For in their turmoil, there's a chance to grow,
To mend the fragments, let forgiveness flow,
To peel back the layers, to truly see,
The flawed beauty that makes them uniquely free.

Through the trials and tribulations they face,
They discover resilience, find solace in grace,
For a complicated relationship holds profound art,
A journey of growth, a chance to restart.

So, let them navigate this intricate terrain,
With open hearts, embracing joy and pain,
For in the depths of their entangled souls,
Lies the possibility to heal, to make each other whole.

In the tapestry of complicated love's embrace,
They find strength in vulnerability, a sacred space,
And as they unravel the knots of their bond,
They emerge stronger, united, and beyond.

Messy Minds

In the depths of thought, where chaos thrives,
A messy mind dances, tangled, alive.
A tempest within, an ocean untamed,
Where overthinking thoughts are unrestrained.

Like a symphony of worries, they arise,
Notes of doubt and fear, painting the skies.
Each question a whirlwind, spinning around,
Till clarity's lost, in the labyrinth found.

The tendrils of overthinking tightly coil,
As ruminations twist and endlessly toil.
What-ifs and maybes, a relentless storm,
Confining the mind, a prison to conform.

Each decision dissected, examined, weighed,
An endless cycle, where peace is betrayed.
Unanswered queries fuel the ceaseless quest,
Seeking solace in answers yet undressed.

Oh, the weariness of this restless mind,
Weaving tales of doubt that are unkind.
But amidst the turmoil, a glimmer resides,
A reminder that within chaos, beauty hides.

For in the depths of a messy mind's embrace,
Creativity blossoms, finding its space.
Through tangled thoughts, new perspectives bloom,
A kaleidoscope of ideas, vibrant and immune.

So let the overthinking storm abate,
Release the need to constantly debate.
Embrace the messiness, the vivid array,
And let your thoughts wander, freely, today.

For in the tapestry of a messy mind's art,
There lies the potential for a brand new start.
A symphony of thoughts, both wild and refined,
Creating magic from the chaos enshrined.

Autumn Leaves

In hues of gold and crimson red,
Autumn leaves gently grace the ground.
Whispering tales of seasons past,
Their fleeting beauty knows no bound.

They dance upon the gentle breeze,
A symphony of rustling sound.
With each twirl and graceful sway,
They paint the world in hues profound.

Nature's tapestry, a masterpiece,
As fall's embrace begins to fade.
But in their fragile, tender descent,
The essence of life's cycle is portrayed.

So let us cherish autumn's gift,
Those leaves that grace the earth below.
For in their quiet, humble fall,
A glimpse of beauty we shall know.

Growing up

In the garden of innocence, I once bloomed,
A tender bud, with dreams yet consumed.
Whispers of youth, like a gentle breeze,
Guided my steps, filled my heart with ease.

But Time, a wise sculptor, began its creation,
Crafting the masterpiece of maturation.
Each passing day, a stroke of growth,
As petals unfurled, revealing truth.

Oh, the sweet taste of curiosity's delight,
As I ventured forth, embracing the light.
The world, a canvas of endless hues,
Waiting for me to paint my own views.

With wide-eyed wonder, I danced through the years,
Chasing dreams, conquering doubts and fears.
The playgrounds of childhood were left behind,
Replaced by the paths where wisdom I'd find.

In the realm of adulthood, responsibility stood,
A gentle teacher, shaping me as it should.
Lessons of resilience, trials faced and overcome,
Forged my character, making me whole, not undone.

I stumbled, I faltered, I made my mistakes,
Yet from each stumble, strength I would take.
For growth does not come without a cost,
But with each fall, a chance to be lost.

Through heartache's rain, and joys' embrace,
I learned the value of time and its pace.
In the tapestry of life, my threads were spun,
Interwoven with love, laughter, and wisdom won.

Now, I stand tall, a tree with roots profound,
Branches reaching up, touching sky's bound.
The child within me still sings and dreams,
But wiser eyes see what the future redeems.

So, let us cherish the journey we've had,
For growing up is not something to be sad.
In the symphony of life, our parts we play,
With grace, we dance, embracing each new day.

Paradise

In lands unseen, where dreams abide,
There lies a place where hearts reside.
A realm of bliss, serene and fair,
A paradise beyond compare.

Amidst the glimmering emerald fields,
Where sunlight dances, joy reveals,
A tapestry of vibrant hues,
Painted by nature, a heavenly muse.

The fragrance of blossoms fills the air,
Whispering secrets, relieving all care.
The melody of birds in harmony,
Lulls the soul into serenity.

Crystal rivers meander through the land,
Reflecting skies, a divine command.
Their gentle ripples, a soothing song,
Inviting all to dance along.

Majestic mountains, their peaks so high,
Touch the heavens, kiss the sky.
They guard the land with steadfast might,
A testament to nature's grand design.

In this paradise, time is but a friend,
A gentle breeze that knows no end.
No worries, no burdens, no fears to weigh,
Just pure elation, day after day.

The inhabitants, with hearts aglow,
Bound by love that continues to grow.
Kindness reigns in every soul,
Nurturing compassion, making it whole.

The laughter of children fills the air,
Their innocence, a treasure rare.
Their smiles, a reflection of pure delight,
In this haven, their spirits take flight.

In paradise, dreams become alive,
As aspirations and passions thrive.
Each soul finds purpose, a divine decree,
A journey of self-discovery.

Oh, how I yearn for this paradise true,
Where love and joy forever renew.
Though distant it may seem, in my heart it resides,
A sanctuary of peace where love abides.

So let us dream, let us believe,
In the paradise we can achieve.
For within our souls, the power lies,
To create a haven, beneath the azure skies.

Poetic Tapestry

In the depths of night, where shadows dance,
A tapestry woven of dreams and chance.
Let me spin a tale in poetic rhyme,
Where words intertwine, a timeless chime.

Beneath a sky adorned with twinkling light,
Whispers of stars paint the canvas of night.
Moonbeams cascade upon the tranquil scene,
As silence beckons, a poet's serene.

Through whispered winds, a symphony begins,
Nature's secrets whispered on softest wings.
The rustling leaves, a gentle lullaby,
As nature's poetry sings from the sky.

Oh, behold the majestic ocean's roar,
As waves crash upon the eternal shore.
Each droplet a story, a tale untold,
Unveiling mysteries, ancient and bold.

In fields of flowers, colors burst and bloom,
A fragrant kiss, dispelling all gloom.
Petals sway to an unseen melody,
Nature's poetry, a sight to see.

And in the depths of a lover's embrace,
A language spoken with a tender grace.
Two souls entwined in an eternal dance,
Whispering verses, their hearts' romance.

In laughter shared, friendships ever true,
An ode to joy, a bond that grew.
Memories etched in hearts, forever treasured,
A testament to love, beyond measure.

So let us wander through this world's embrace,
With open hearts, embracing every trace.
For life itself is poetry profound,
In every sight, every whispering sound.

In every moment, a verse to be found,
In every heartbeat, a rhythm unbound.
Let us be poets, with souls set free,
In this vast universe of poetry.

Hopeful Dreams Unite

Amidst the chaos that surrounds,
Where troubles seem to grow,
A melody of hope resounds,
Embracing hearts with a glow.

Let's dream of a brighter tomorrow,
Where unity shall prevail,
Where love dissolves all sorrow,
And kindness will never fail.

In this tapestry of endless dreams,
A symphony of change will play,
A world where equality redeems,
And justice guides the way.

Let bridges mend and walls break down,
As empathy takes its stance,
Together we'll erase the frown,
With open hearts and a chance.

For every seed of hope we sow,
A garden of compassion will bloom,
A future where all hearts will know,
The beauty in each soul's resume.

Let's paint a world of vibrant hues,
Where dreams can truly ignite,
Where courage triumphs and love ensues,
Igniting a future so bright.

So let us rise, hand in hand,
And march towards that distant shore,
Where hope shines like golden sand,
And a better future we'll explore.

Black & White Yearning

In a world of vibrant hues, I yearn to be,
Lost in the charm of a black and white movie.
Where shadows dance upon a silver screen,
And love's allure is eternally pristine.

I wish to wander through cobblestone streets,
With a vintage hat and a heart that beats,
In sync with the melodies of a bygone age,
Where passion ignites with a timeless stage.

In monochrome splendor, I would reside,
In a realm where emotions need not hide.
Where subtle glances speak volumes untold,
And whispered words are worth more than gold.

Let me step into frames of celluloid grace,
Where love blooms gently in each tender embrace.
With wistful eyes and a touch so divine,
We'd waltz through moments, frozen in time.

I'd stroll beneath the glow of dim streetlights,
Hand in hand, with my love through the nights.
Raindrops would kiss our umbrella's embrace,
As we twirl through the rhythm of a silver chase.

Oh, how I long for that classic allure,
Where love's essence is pure and demure.
In a realm where every moment's a work of art,
Where the black and white canvas captures my heart.

Yet, amidst the shades of gray, I'd find,
A love that's vibrant, unbreakable, and kind.
For in this monochromatic reverie,
Love's palette would paint in hues unseen.

Let me dwell in that dreamer's sphere,
A black and white movie, so vivid and clear.
Where romance blossoms, never to fade,
In a world where true love has always been made.

Forest Symphony

In the heart of nature's verdant domain,
Where ancient trees sway, a wild refrain,
I woke, mid-forest, as the dawn did rise,
Enraptured by the chorus of avian skies.

From slumber's embrace, I gently awoke,
To whispers of leaves, their rustling spoke,
The morning sun's caress on mossy ground,
As melodies of birds in joy resound.

In dappled light, their wings adorned with hue,
A symphony of notes, both old and new,
Each feathered troubadour their song did lend,
A magical sonnet, nature's gift to send.

The robin's trill, a sweet and mirthful sound,
The lark's ascent, a soulful echo found,
And in the distance, the woodpecker's beat,
A rhythmic pulse, with nature's heartbeat meet.

Amongst the ancient oaks, tall and proud,
I stood, in awe, beneath their leafy shroud,
And as I listened to the birdsong's tale,
I felt my spirit soar, my heart exhale.

For in that moment, time had lost its way,
And all the worries of the world did sway,
As nature's poets serenaded me,
A captive audience in this symphony.

Oh, woodland choir, your voices interweave,
As if to teach the lost how to believe,
In harmony and unity of all,
The language spoken when the bird's notes fall.

So let me linger here, midst verdant lore,
Where ancient secrets lie, forevermore,
Awake in the embrace of nature's boughs,
Imbued with peace, as morning's light allows.

In this enchanted forest, I shall stay,
To listen to the birds, their songs convey,
And let their melodies guide me along,
As I awaken to the world's sweet song.

My Muse

In the realm where dreams take flight,
Where inspiration weaves its light,
There exists a muse, ethereal and rare,
A source of wonder beyond compare.

A symphony of words, her gentle voice,
A whispered melody, my heart's own choice.
Her eyes, like stars in the midnight sky,
Hold secrets untold, the reasons why.

She dances through the fields of thought,
A sprite, a guide, with grace she's brought,
With every step, she paints the air,
Transforming moments, weaving flair.

In her presence, colors bloom and blend,
A tapestry of emotions, where souls transcend,
Her laughter rings, a soft cascading stream,
And echoes of joy, in every dream.

She stirs the embers of my restless mind,
Igniting flames, burning bright, entwined.
Her touch, a gentle breeze upon my skin,
Awakening dormant thoughts deep within.

Through her eyes, I see the world anew,
A kaleidoscope of beauty, ever true.
She inspires the poet's ink to flow,
With each word crafted, her essence grows.

Oh, muse of mine, enchantress divine,
You've unlocked the gate to realms sublime,
I'm but a vessel, a vessel for your art,
Bound by the spell you cast upon my heart.

For in your presence, I find my voice,
And through your essence, I rejoice.
In this dance of creation, we are entwined,
Forever bound, muse of my mind.

Sunflower

In fields of gold where sunshine gleams,
A radiant flower, a poet's dreams,
The sunflower stands with vibrant grace,
A golden emblem, nature's embrace.

With slender stalks, they reach so high,
Yearning for warmth in the vast blue sky.
Their faces follow the sun's golden trail,
From dawn's first blush to twilight's veil.

Petals like rays in a vibrant array,
Bathing in sunlight, their spirits sway,
Bold and bright, a burst of yellow hue,
They dance with joy, their souls renewed.

Their hearts, a spiral of secrets hold,
Whispering tales from days of old,
Each petal, a verse, a story to tell,
Of nature's wisdom, they speak so well.

In summer's breeze, they gently sway,
Serenading bees, inviting them to play,
Their nectar, a sweet ambrosial treat,
Nourishing life with each sun-kissed feat.

Amidst the fields, a symphony unfolds,
Where sunflowers stand, their secrets untold,
A chorus of beauty, a sight to behold,
A masterpiece painted in petals of gold.

Oh, sunflower, emblem of the sun,
Teaching us lessons, one by one,
To seek the light and face the day,
To bloom with grace, come what may.

As seasons change and years pass by,
The sunflower stands, tall and spry,
A symbol of hope, resilience, and grace,
Forever blooming, in every space.

Learn from this radiant flower,
To face the world with courage and power,
Embrace the sunlight, let our spirits rise,
Just like the sunflower, reaching for the skies.

Mind Games

In the realm where thoughts collide,
Where whispers of truth and shadows reside,
There lies a playground, mysterious and vast,
Where the mind games begin, a captivating contrast.

Oh, the tricks the mind can play,
Leading us astray, in a delicate ballet,
Illusions dancing with cunning grace,
Challenging perceptions, a mystical chase.

Within this labyrinth, perceptions twist,
Riddles and enigmas, a mind's tryst,
Thoughts entwined in a complex maze,
A perplexing journey, a captivating craze.

A symphony of ideas, both bright and dark,
Whispers of reason, a relentless embark,
In the depths of consciousness, secrets hide,
Like puzzles awaiting to be untied.

One moment, clarity's radiant light,
Guiding the way through the darkest night,
Yet in the next breath, confusion's embrace,
Leading us deeper into this perplexing space.

Oh, the intricate dance of the mind's ballet,
Leading us astray, as realities sway,
Mirrors reflecting fragmented reflections,
A tapestry of truths and deceiving inflections.

Beware the illusions, the mind's wicked game,
For it knows no boundaries, no sense of shame,
It weaves its web with cunning threads,
Blurring the lines where sanity treads.

But amidst the chaos, a wisdom takes flight,
A resilience born from the mind's eternal fight,
Through introspection, we learn to discern,
The illusions that bewitch, the truths we yearn.

So, let us embrace these mind games profound,
As we unravel the mysteries that surround,
For within the enigma lies wisdom's domain,
Where the mind's labyrinth shall never wane.

Beauty & The Beast

In a realm where contrasts collide,
A tale of Beauty and Beast does reside.
An enchanting fable of love's sweet dance,
Where outward appearances yearn for a chance.

Beauty, a rose amidst a garden fair,
Graceful and gentle, beyond compare.
Her heart, a beacon of kindness and light,
Unveiling true beauty, shining so bright.

The Beast, a figure shrouded in gloom,
With fur and fangs, a visage of doom.
Yet within his fortress, a longing soul,
Scarred and wounded, seeking to feel whole.

Their paths intertwined by destiny's hand,
Two worlds colliding in a mystical land.
Fear and curiosity, swirling with might,
They embark on a journey, day and night.

Beyond the surface, they start to see,
A connection blooming, setting them free.
For true beauty resides in hearts untamed,
In compassion and love, forever unchained.

As the Beast reveals his tender core,
Beauty embraces him, cherishing more.
She sees not the monster, but a wounded soul,
Seeking redemption, a chance to be whole.

With each passing moment, love takes root,
Transforming their lives, casting off the brute.
The Beast's rough edges begin to refine,
Under Beauty's touch, he starts to shine.

In the garden of their love's sweet refrain,
Petals of hope and forgiveness remain.
They dance through darkness, hand in hand,
A bond unbreakable, steadfastly grand.

For love, in its essence, sees beyond guise,
It pierces the veil, where true beauty lies.
The Beauty and Beast, a story profound,
Where inner radiance eternally astounds.

Camping in the wild

In the heart of untamed nature's embrace,
Where the spirit of adventure finds its place,
Amidst the wilderness, untouched and grand,
We embark on a journey, hand in hand.

Beneath the starlit canopy, so vast,
Camping in the wild, our souls hold fast,
The crackling fire, a flickering light,
Guiding our stories through the peaceful night.

The earthy scent of pine fills the air,
As the breeze whispers secrets, we're aware,
Of ancient tales woven in each tree,
And the untold wonders yet to be free.

The moon, a radiant beacon above,
Casts its glow, revealing nature's love,
A symphony of nocturnal creatures' song,
Echoing through valleys, serene and strong.

With each breath, we taste the wilderness true,
And embrace the freedom that it imbues,
The weight of the world, it fades away,
In this haven of nature, where we play.

We pitch our tents, like humble abodes,
Amidst meadows, rivers, and mountain roads,
Nature's canvas, adorned with vibrant hues,
A masterpiece painted with a gentle muse.

As dawn breaks, painting the sky with gold,
We witness nature's wonders, yet untold,
The playful dance of sunlight through the leaves,
As wilderness awakens and new life conceives.

We venture forth, exploring the unknown,
Trails unmarked, but nature's map is sown,
Discovering hidden gems along the way,
As we surrender to nature's grand display.

By nightfall, we gather, hearts full and bright,
Around the campfire, our souls take flight,
Underneath a blanket of stars above,
We find solace in wild nature's love.

And when our journey comes to an end,
We leave no trace, our promise to defend,
For nature's sanctuary, a sacred space,
Preserved for generations, its embrace.

So, let us venture into the wild unknown,
Where camping in nature becomes our own,
With every step, we find our souls set free,
Embracing the wild, where we're meant to be.

Running with the wind

In fields of dreams, where freedom's found,
Where whispers echo without a sound,
There lies a soul unbound, untamed,
Running with the wind, unrestrained.

Beneath the vast and endless sky,
Where dreams take flight, and spirits fly,
A symphony of pure liberation plays,
As I dance with the breeze in joyful displays.

My feet meet earth's tender embrace,
As I surrender to nature's grace,
Every step a rhythm, every breath a song,
In this world of liberation, I belong.

No chains to bind, no limits to confine,
I chase the sun, a soul aligned,
With every stride, I leave behind,
The burdens that my heart resigned.

Through open meadows, I gracefully glide,
Embracing the currents, I become one with the tide,
The whispers of the grass, a gentle refrain,
As freedom's symphony weaves through my veins.

The wind, my companion, a spirited guide,
Through valleys and mountains, side by side,
Together we soar, fearless and free,
Unleashing the wild spirit within me.

With each passing moment, my spirit ascends,
Boundaries blurred, limitations transcends,
For in this realm, where dreams take flight,
I am liberated, in purest delight.

So let us run, run with the wind,
Feel the rush, let our souls be pinned,
To the canvas of the sky, in vibrant hues,
As freedom's spirit ignites and renews.

For in the boundless embrace of nature's realm,
We find the essence of life's overwhelming helm,
And in this poetry of liberation and zest,
Our souls find solace, forever blessed.

Inner Power

In the depths of our being, a spark resides,
A flicker of light that within us abides.
It's the ember of belief, fierce and bold,
The essence that guides us, as life unfolds.

In a world filled with doubt and constant strife,
We often forget the power within our life.
But hear me now, with heartfelt decree,
Belief in oneself sets the spirit free.

When storms assail and clouds loom above,
And dreams seem distant, lost in the cove,
Remember the strength that lies in your core,
Believe in yourself, and you shall soar.

For belief is the foundation that paves the way,
To triumphs and victories, come what may.
It fuels the courage to chase our desires,
To scale the mountains, to ignite the fires.

In moments of darkness, when shadows encroach,
Doubt may whisper, leaving us reproach.
But hold steadfast to the belief you possess,
For it shall lead you through the abyss's distress.

Believe in your worth, for you are unique,
With talents and passions, ready to speak.
Embrace your potential, let your spirit shine,
For within you, the extraordinary shall align.

Trust in your dreams, let them dance and unfurl,
With belief as your guide, watch them swirl.
No hurdle too high, no goal out of sight,
With unwavering belief, you shall take flight.

In the tapestry of life, we each have a role,
Believing in ourselves, we become whole.
So, nurture that flame, let it burn and ignite,
For within you, my friend, lies infinite might.

Believe, oh believe, in your infinite worth,
For the universe listens, embracing your birth.
With faith in your heart, you'll transcend every test,
And live a life fulfilled, truly at your best.

Thank you for reading me!

:)

Printed in Great Britain
by Amazon

24426271R00040